FROM DEBT TO FREEDOM

A JOURNEY THROUGH BANKRUPTCY

A Personal Journey

Seawife Smith

White Cedar Quill Press

Author: Seawife Smith

ISBN 978-1-7638546-0-4

Contact email: seawife@mail.com

Printed in Australia – January 2025

"From Debt to Freedom: A Journey through Bankruptcy"

This book is a deeply personal and emotional account of the struggles and triumphs of facing unmanageable debt and navigating the life-changing process of bankruptcy. Written in the first person, it delves into the crushing weight of sleepless nights, the endless cycle of fear and desperation, and the agonizing choices that debt forces upon us.

Through raw honesty, it uncovers how life's unexpected turns, a job loss, a family crisis, or even the love of a beloved pet, can spiral into financial ruin. But it's also a story of resilience. From the first steps of confronting the mounting bills to the liberating moment of bankruptcy approval, and ultimately, the bittersweet lessons learned along the way, this book offers hope to anyone drowning in debt.

The narrative strips away the stigma of bankruptcy, showing it as not an end but a chance to rebuild. It shares practical insights into the process, from completing forms to understanding the financial consequences, while weaving in the emotional toll, and eventual relief, of finally letting go of the fear.

In these pages, readers will find a relatable voice, a roadmap out of despair, and a reminder that even in the darkest times, there is a path to recovery. Bankruptcy is not a failure; it's an opportunity for a fresh start, and this book shows how to embrace it with courage and hope.

Perfect for anyone seeking understanding, solace, or the strength to begin again.

Table of Contents

Chapter 1: The First Calls

The Debt Trap

The first time the phone rang, I ignored it. Unknown numbers always felt like a gamble, and besides, I had more pressing things to worry about, like how I was going to stretch my dwindling pay to cover rent, utilities, and food for the month. But when it rang again, and then again, I knew it wasn't a coincidence.

"*This is a courtesy call regarding your overdue balance*" the voice on the other end said, polite but firm. My stomach twisted into knots as I mumbled an apology and hung up. That's when it began: the calls, the letters, the gnawing sense of dread that followed me everywhere. It was as if my debts had grown legs and started chasing me down, demanding a reckoning I wasn't ready to face.

At first, I told myself it was a temporary setback. I'd find a way to catch up, to juggle the overdue bills with the ones still piling up. But deep down, I knew. The math didn't add up. No matter how many times I scribbled numbers on scraps of paper, there was always more owed than earned. And yet, it hadn't always been this way.

The Beginning of the End

The first debt was small. It seemed almost laughable now, a hundred dollars borrowed to cover a veterinarian bill for Max, my golden retriever dog. He had gotten sick unexpectedly, and the sight of him lying weak and motionless on the floor was unbearable. The vet's eyes were kind but unyielding: *"We'll need to run some tests. It could be serious."*

That moment marked the beginning of a nightmare I couldn't have foreseen. The prognosis came back grim: Max had ingested snail baits from the neighbour's garden, and the toxins had caused acute kidney failure. The vet explained the options: *"We'll try to flush the toxins out, but it's going to take days of treatment, constant monitoring, and intravenous fluids. There's a chance, but it's 50/50."*

I couldn't let him die without a fight. I would have sold my soul if it meant saving him. He was more than a pet; he was my best friend, my constant companion through some of the hardest days of my life. Max had been there when no one else was, wagging his tail when I came home, nudging me out of bed when the weight of the world felt too heavy.

When others told me, *"It's kinder to put him down,"* their words were like knives. How could I give up on him? Max was family, and you don't abandon family when they're suffering.

What followed were days of desperation. Max was hooked up to an IV drip, his frail body lying still on a blanket in the sterile vet clinic. There were blood tests, endless rounds of medicines, painkillers, and glimmers of false hope every time he wagged his tail or opened his eyes. I sat beside him for hours, whispering words of encouragement he likely couldn't hear but I needed to say.

Every day, the vet bills piled higher. My credit card became my lifeline, swiped again and again as the totals grew into the thousands. *"We'll try one more day,"* I'd say to myself, clutching to hope like a lifeline, convinced that tomorrow might bring a miracle. But with every passing day, the vet's face grew more sombre, and the odds slipped further away.

Finally, after days of watching him fight, the vet pulled me aside. *"The damage is extensive,"* he said gently. *"There's nothing more we can do. It's time to take him home and let him rest."* I felt like the world crumbled around me. I brought Max back home, wrapped in his favourite blanket, and laid him in his bed by the window where he loved to sit. I spent the last days with him, stroking his fur and telling him it was okay to let go. When he took his final breath, I felt a grief so deep it was as though I had lost a part of myself.

The house felt empty without him. The quiet was unbearable. I had spent thousands of dollars, money I didn't have, on a losing battle, but I couldn't regret it. Max had been worth every cent, every sleepless night, every tear. But that decision marked the first step down a path I never imagined I'd walk.

I had started with a small debt. It felt manageable at first. I told myself I could pay it off next month, but next month came, and something else demanded attention, a car repair I couldn't put off. One necessity snowballed into another, and the minimum payments became a game of musical chairs. My credit cards were maxed, the balances crept higher, and soon, I was borrowing to pay off what I had already borrowed. It was like a tidal wave slowly building, and I couldn't stop it.

Max's loss was more than emotional; it was financial. And though the grief eventually became bearable, the debt remained, growing heavier with time.

And then came the breaking point: I lost my job. A restructuring, they called it, as if rearranging the pieces on a board absolved them of the lives it upended. I'd spent weeks sending out resumes, smiling through interviews, trying to project the confidence I no longer felt. But the bills didn't wait. Rent was due. Groceries needed buying. And when the credit cards ran out, payday loans filled the gap, predatory lifelines that pulled me deeper into the abyss.

A System on the Brink

It's a quiet truth no one wants to admit: most of us are only a pay away from disaster. A job loss, an illness, a car accident, or even an unexpected birth can tip the scales. The safety nets we imagine we have, savings, insurance, even friends and family, are rarely as sturdy as we believe. My family tried to help at first. My mom paid my utility bill one month. My brother sent me grocery money another month. But their resources were limited too. "*We can't keep doing this*" they said, their voices tinged with guilt and frustration.

The strain on our relationships was immediate and palpable. Family gatherings became tense. Conversations skirted around my struggles, avoiding the obvious truth: I had become a burden. Offers of help turned into arguments, each party grappling with the limits of their generosity. And then, one by one, they pulled away, not out of malice, but self-preservation.

The Weight of the World

Debt is insidious that way. It isolates you, makes you feel like you're the only one drowning while everyone else is swimming effortlessly. But the truth is, there are millions like me, living pay to pay, hoping nothing catastrophic happens. Divorce, for instance, can tear not just a family apart but also a financial foundation. Medical emergencies often leave people with a choice: save a loved one or lose everything. And single mothers, abandoned or unsupported, are left juggling the impossible task of raising a child and surviving on their own.

Each debt adds another brick to the load, until one day, it becomes too heavy to carry. The calls turn into threats, the letters into warnings of legal action. Eviction notices appear on doors. People are forced to make impossible choices: heat or food, rent or medicine. And for too many, the end of the line is homelessness, a place where debt stops being numbers on a page and becomes the lived reality of cold nights and endless uncertainty.

A Glimpse of Hope

I'd like to say I found a way out, that the calls stopped, and the knots in my stomach loosened. But life isn't that simple. What I can say is that I'm still here, still fighting. Every day is a battle against despair, but it's also a reminder of what's at stake. And maybe, just maybe, there's a way forward. But for now, the phone keeps ringing.

Chapter 2: The Spiral

Desperate Options

The stress became a constant companion. While employed, it followed me to work, where I struggled to focus, and it kept me up at night, staring at the ceiling, my mind racing with "what ifs." What if they garnished my wages? What if I lost my apartment? What if everyone found out? Once I lost my job the stress multiplied. My mind became a battlefield, with endless scenarios of failure and desperation playing on repeat.

Some nights, I found myself pacing, desperate to find a solution. I'd scribble lists of options in the dark: Should I sell my car? What if I sold everything I owned? I had a mortgage on a small house, a place I'd once been proud of, but I was behind on payments. Selling it might clear a portion of my debt, but then what? Where would I go?

I thought about moving in with family, but things between us were already strained. Pride, shame, and the fear of being a burden kept me from picking up the phone. Couch surfing was an option, but only if I could find someone willing to take me in.

And what about people who had no one to call? People without friends or family? What did they do?

I wondered if I could live in my car. I'd heard stories of people who showered at gyms, who parked in safe neighbourhoods, working whatever jobs they could find while sleeping in the backseat. I thought about tents in parks, about people who had no choice but to lay down roots wherever they could, braving the elements with nothing but a tarp overhead. How close was I to that life?

"Maybe I can get government assistance," I told myself one night. But how long would that take? Months, probably. Emergency housing programs existed, but the demand far outstripped the supply. I didn't qualify for most programs yet, but I knew I was skirting dangerously close to that line. Social security, food stamps, rent assistance, all of these floated through my mind like lifeboats just out of reach.

When you're drowning in debt, your mind becomes a battleground. Every decision feels desperate, every plan is flawed. Sell the house? Move out and live in my car? Rent a storage unit and sleep on the floor? The thoughts circled endlessly, growing more frantic as the nights stretched on. And the less I slept, the more my world unravelled. Sleep deprivation does funny things to a person. It makes you paranoid, hopeless, and irrational.

On my darkest nights, I felt like I was the only one in the world going through this. Rationally, I knew that wasn't true. I'd read stories about people who lost everything, a job, a spouse, a home, and ended up on the streets. But when you're in the thick of it, your problems feel singular and insurmountable.

I thought about people without homes, the people I passed on my way to work, bundled under thin blankets, their belongings stuffed into plastic bags. Once, I might have judged them. Now, I saw the truth: they were me, just a step further down the path.

And the calls kept coming.

The collectors' tactics became more aggressive. The once-polite calls turned sharper, their tone tinged with a mix of authority and disdain. "*We can set up a payment plan*" they'd suggest, as if I hadn't already tried that. They didn't understand that there was nothing left to give. Every dollar was accounted for before it even hit my account.

And then there were the letters. They came in plain envelopes, their stark black print spelling out numbers I couldn't bear to read. I shoved them into a drawer, thinking if I didn't open them, maybe the problem would disappear. But debt doesn't vanish when ignored. It festers, growing bigger and uglier until it's impossible to avoid.

Desperation hung over me like a storm cloud, and I realised that no matter how many lists I made, no matter how many options I considered, I couldn't see a way out. My choices weren't choices at all. They were just different shades of loss.

Owning a Home but Losing Control

For some people, debt starts to erode the very ground they stand on, their homes. I thought about those with mortgages who faced the terrible question: should I sell the house? Could I even find a buyer fast enough to stop the flood? Selling might stave off the collectors for a while, but where would they go next? And then the fear: What if I'm stuck paying the mortgage for a house I no longer even own?

For renters like me, the questions weren't easier. Falling behind on rent felt like standing on a crumbling ledge. Should I pack up and leave before eviction forced me out? Should I move into my car, or worse, pitch a tent in the park? I couldn't help but think of those who had no car, no tent, and no choice but to wander.

Turning to Family and Temporary Help

Some have family to lean on, or at least to ask. The idea of moving in with my parents crossed my mind. I imagined the awkward dinners, the silent shame of needing to rely on them. Would they even understand the weight I carried? Relationships are strained under financial stress, and I knew that living under the same roof again might split us apart completely.

Then there was the thought of couch surfing, bouncing between friends' houses like a ghost. For a while, it might work, but what about those who didn't have friends or family to ask? I realised how fragile support systems can be and how easy it is to fall through the cracks.

Seeking Government Assistance: Questions Without Answers

I started researching emergency assistance, only to be faced with a wall of uncertainty. Could I apply for

Social Security or other benefits to bridge the gap? How long would it take to get approval? Months? Years? Could I afford to wait that long? What about emergency housing? There were programs, sure, but there were also waiting lists, and those lists were long.

I thought about the stories I'd heard of people sleeping in shelters or waiting for a miracle that never came. The system, while designed to help, often moves at a pace too slow for those who are drowning. Each call I made, each webpage I read, seemed to add more questions than answers.

The Desperation of No Options

When you're faced with debt and uncertainty, your mind becomes a maze of impossible choices. Sell everything and start over? Move somewhere cheaper, even if it meant sacrificing safety? Apply for aid that might never come? My mind spiralled as the walls closed in. For every idea that surfaced, ten new obstacles appeared.

Debt strips away your ability to dream, leaving only survival. And for the first time, I began to understand the depths of hopelessness that lead people to homelessness. For those without options, there's no safety net, just freefall.

Living With Uncertainty

The sleepless nights became longer, and the weight of my situation grew heavier. My mind never rested, constantly calculating, constantly searching for a solution that didn't exist. What I didn't know at the time was that these feelings, the desperation, the uncertainty, were shared by so many others. I wasn't alone, but it certainly felt like I was.

And in those darkest hours, as I sat awake in the dead of night, I wondered: how much longer could I hold on before everything fell apart completely?

Chapter 3: The Fear of Bankruptcy

Bankruptcy: A Word We Fear

Even as my debts spiralled further out of control, I couldn't bear to consider bankruptcy. That single word, bankruptcy, held so much stigma, so much weight. It was the word the news warned you about, the fate whispered about when someone in town "lost it all." It felt like an admission of failure, a permanent scar on my record. The media painted bankruptcy as a horror story: homes lost, reputations destroyed, credit scores shattered beyond repair.

For days, I tried to ignore the possibility. Bankruptcy felt like defeat, a last resort that would mark me as irresponsible and careless. But the deeper I sank, the more impossible it became to ignore. I had to know: what would it really mean to declare bankruptcy? Was it as terrifying as I'd been led to believe?

Seeking Stories in the Shadows

Late one night, with my heart pounding and tears in my eyes, I opened my laptop and began searching for answers. I typed, hesitantly at first: "What happens when you file for bankruptcy?" What I found surprised me. Among the articles warning of financial ruin were stories from real people, people like me, who had been there.

There were mothers drowning in medical debt after a child's illness. Fathers who lost jobs and couldn't keep up with the mortgage. Young professionals buried under student loans they could never repay. I read about how they, too, had feared bankruptcy, how they felt it would ruin them. But to my surprise, most of them said the same thing: bankruptcy wasn't the end. It was a new beginning.

Peeling Away the Fear

The more I read, the more I realised that much of my fear came from misinformation. Bankruptcy wasn't some great punishment for the wicked; it was a legal tool, a reset button for people who had nowhere else to turn. Yes, there would be consequences, credit scores would take a hit, assets might be lost, but there was also freedom on the other side.

I found stories of people who had rebuilt their lives. Some rented apartments, saving slowly until they could buy a home again. Others started new careers, untethered from the weight of past debts. Their stories gave me hope.

The Weight of Shame

Still, the shame lingered. How could I face my family and friends if I chose this path? Would they think less of me? Would I lose their respect? I imagined the whispers: "*She went bankrupt. She must have been reckless*".

For many of us drowning in debt, shame is the heaviest burden of all. We think we are alone, that we're somehow to blame for every bad break, every mistake. But as I kept reading, I realised something: life happens. Jobs are lost, people get sick, marriages fall apart. Sometimes, no matter how hard you work, it's not enough.

Bankruptcy wasn't about blaming myself, it was about finding a way out.

Research and Reality

Over the next few days, I kept researching. I learned about different types of bankruptcy, about repayment plans, and about fresh starts. I discovered that, yes, bankruptcy would stay on my credit report for years, but that didn't mean I could never rebuild. I read practical advice about budgeting after bankruptcy, how to live within my means, and how to start again with small, achievable goals.

As I absorbed all this information, something shifted. Bankruptcy was no longer a monster lurking in the dark. It was a doorway, one I was beginning to believe I could walk through.

Making the Decision

The decision didn't come easily. I wrestled with it, questioned it, and second-guessed myself at every turn. But the more I weighed my options, the clearer it became. I couldn't keep living like this, the sleepless nights, the constant anxiety, the hopelessness. Bankruptcy, as terrifying as it seemed, offered me something I hadn't felt in years: hope.

By the end of that week, I made up my mind. I would explore this path, not as a failure, but as someone ready to take control of their life again.

For the first time in months, I felt something close to relief. The fear wasn't completely gone, but it was no longer paralysing. I didn't know what the future would look like, but I knew one thing: I was ready to take the first step.

Chapter 4: Finding Help

The Reluctance to Ask for Help

Admitting that I needed help was one of the hardest parts of this journey. For so long, I had carried the weight of my debt in silence, believing that I could somehow manage to dig myself out of the hole on my own. The thought of asking for help felt like admitting defeat, a sign that I had truly failed. On top of that, there was the stigma, bankruptcy was something I associated with shame and ruin. My mind was clouded with fears: What will people think? Will I lose everything? Will I ever recover from this?

I spent days avoiding the inevitable, pacing around my apartment as I tried to convince myself that there was still another way. Maybe if I could pick up a second job, sell more things, or somehow cut back on expenses even further. But deep down, I knew I was already at my limit. I was exhausted, mentally and physically, from carrying the burden. Something had to change.

Where Do I Even Start?

Once I began to consider bankruptcy, a new kind of panic set in: Where do I start? Who do I talk to? I had no legal knowledge, no idea what the process entailed, or even what the first step was. The word *bankruptcy* felt huge, overwhelming, and impossible to grasp. I imagined courtrooms, endless forms, and a bureaucratic nightmare I wasn't equipped to face. My confidence was already at rock bottom, how could I possibly navigate such a complicated process alone?

I started researching late at night, scrolling through financial forums, articles, and personal blogs. I read stories from people who had gone through bankruptcy, clinging to any hint of advice or guidance they could offer. Some stories were reassuring, but others painted a picture of confusion and frustration. The more I read, the more I realised that I couldn't do this alone. I needed someone to guide me.

Finding Free Financial Counsellors

One late night, while searching for help online, I stumbled upon a small glimmer of hope: free financial counselling services. I learned that many local communities offer financial counsellors who provide free advice and support for those struggling with debt. These counsellors weren't lawyers or judgmental figures, they were people trained to help individuals like me navigate through the storm. The idea of free help felt like a lifeline. I couldn't afford expensive legal advice, so this seemed like the only way forward.

I hesitated before reaching out. I worried that even speaking to someone about bankruptcy would make it more real, that I would be judged for allowing my situation to get so bad. But I had to push past the fear. After days of debating, I finally picked up the phone and called a local non-profit offering financial counselling. The voice on the other end was calm and reassuring. They listened to my story, my worries, and my questions without a hint of judgment. For the first time, I felt like I wasn't entirely alone.

Downloading the Forms: Facing the Paperwork

The financial counsellor explained the steps I needed to take and recommended I start by downloading the bankruptcy forms. I stared at the forms on my computer screen, daunted by their size and complexity. Each page was filled with questions that felt invasive, asking for detailed information about my income, debts, assets, and expenses. Seeing it all in black and white forced me to confront the reality of my situation, there was no hiding from the numbers anymore.

I printed the forms and set them on my kitchen table. For days, they sat there untouched, a looming reminder of what I had to do. I knew that filling them out would mean revisiting every financial mistake I'd made, line by line, and I wasn't sure I was ready for that. But eventually, I realised that procrastinating would only make things worse. I needed to take action, no matter how difficult it was.

Filling in the Details: A Step-by-Step Process

Filling out the bankruptcy forms was a painstaking process. I spent hours going over bank statements, bills, and pay stubs to make sure I answered every question accurately. The forms asked for a complete breakdown of my finances, things I had avoided looking at for months. I had to list every creditor, every debt, and every source of income, no matter how small.

There were moments when I felt completely overwhelmed. I wanted to give up more than once, especially when the questions became harder to answer. How much did I spend on food last month? What assets do I still own? How much is my car worth? Each question forced me to confront the reality of how far I'd fallen, and it wasn't easy.

Seeking Help from Friends and Family

At one point, I broke down. I couldn't do it alone anymore. I called a close friend and asked if they could help me go through the paperwork. It wasn't an easy call to make, I felt embarrassed to admit that I needed help with something so personal, but my friend was kind and understanding. He sat with me at the kitchen table, helping me make sense of the forms and reassuring me when I got overwhelmed.

I also reached out to a family member who had experience managing finances. He gave me practical advice and helped me double-check my numbers. It wasn't easy letting people see the full extent of my financial struggles, but their support gave me the strength to keep going.

The Emotional Toll of the Process

Filling out the bankruptcy paperwork took days, and by the end, I felt drained. The process forced me to relive the past, to see in painful detail how my situation had spiralled out of control. It was a humbling experience, one that left me questioning every decision I'd made. But it was also strangely liberating. For the first time, I wasn't running from my problems. I was confronting them head-on.

I began to see the paperwork as more than just a bureaucratic hurdle. It was a map of where I'd been, but also a path to where I could go next. Each question I answered brought me one step closer to relief, to a chance at starting over.

Moving Forward with Cautious Hope

Once the forms were complete, I felt a small sense of accomplishment. It was just the beginning of the bankruptcy process, but it was a step forward, a step I had taken on my own, with the help of those I trusted. The fear that had paralysed me for so long began to fade, replaced by a cautious hope. I still didn't know what the future would look like, but I knew I couldn't go back to where I'd been.

Reaching out for help, downloading the forms, and filling them in had been some of the hardest steps I'd ever taken. But they were necessary. The process wasn't easy, and it wasn't quick, but for the first time in a long time, I felt like I was finally moving in the right direction.

The Lesson in Asking for Help

If there was one thing I learned during this part of the journey, it was that asking for help isn't a sign of weakness. It's an act of courage. Reaching out to financial counsellors, friends, and family showed me that I wasn't alone, even when I felt like I was. Bankruptcy may be a personal process, but it doesn't mean you have to face it completely on your own.

For anyone considering bankruptcy, the process might seem impossible at first. The forms, the questions, and the shame can feel overwhelming. But taking that first step, no matter how small, can make all the difference. Help is out there. You just have to be willing to ask for it.

By the time I finished this journey, I had taken the first real step toward reclaiming my life. The road ahead was still uncertain, but for the first time, I wasn't paralysed by fear. I had a plan, and I had hope.

Chapter 5: The Final Submission

The Relief of Completion

Finally, after days of painstaking work, I had completed the bankruptcy form. The pages that had once felt like an impossible mountain to climb were now filled in, checked, and double-checked. Alongside the form were the required attachments: bank statements, proof of income, bills, and lists of creditors. I had sourced every piece of documentation they requested, and with a sigh of relief, I sat back and stared at the towering stack of paper that represented my financial life. It wasn't perfect, but it was done, *finally done*.

There was a strange calm in knowing I had done everything I could. The countless hours spent deciphering the questions, gathering the paperwork, and revisiting my financial mistakes had taken an emotional toll, but completing the form marked the end of one chapter and the tentative start of another.

The Unexpected Hurdle: Uploading the Form

Submitting the form was supposed to be the final, simple step, or so I thought. I logged onto the bankruptcy office's website late that night, determined to get it over with. I followed the instructions carefully, attaching the form and its various supporting documents. But when I clicked "upload," an error message flashed across the screen: **File too large.**

I sat frozen, my heart sinking into my stomach. "*No, no, no*" I muttered, staring at the screen as if willing it to change. I tried splitting the documents into smaller parts and re-uploading them piece by piece, but the website rejected every attempt. Hours ticked by, and frustration began to bubble over. It felt like a cruel joke, that after all my hard work, a technical glitch was standing in my way.

I went to bed that night in a haze of exhaustion, my mind racing. Had I come this far only to be stopped by something so small? Would this delay cause more problems? The uncertainty crept back in, gnawing at me. I tossed and turned, running through every possible solution until morning finally came.

Calling for Help: A Solution

The next day, I decided to call the bankruptcy office. I had resisted reaching out before, thinking that admitting I was struggling would somehow reflect badly on me, but now I had no choice. I dialled the number with trembling hands, half-expecting to be met with judgment or disinterest.

To my surprise, the person on the other end was calm and kind. I explained my situation, nervously stumbling over my words, but they reassured me right away. "*It happens more often than you think*" they said. "*Sometimes the file size is just too large for the system to handle. The best solution is to print everything out and bring it to us in person*".

Print it out? Bring it in person? I hadn't expected such an old-fashioned workaround, but at least it was a solution. I felt a wave of relief. I thanked them profusely, grabbed my bag, and set to work.

A Trip to the Bankruptcy Office

Printing everything took longer than I expected. I stood by the printer for what felt like an eternity, watching page after page slowly slide into the tray. The stack was enormous, many pages that held the record of my struggles and failures. I bundled the documents into a folder, double-checked that nothing was missing, and headed out the door.

Walking into the bankruptcy office was a surreal experience. The building itself was non-descript, a plain government office that I might have passed a hundred times without noticing. But as I stepped through the doors, I felt like I was crossing a line I couldn't uncross.

The clerk behind the counter greeted me with a professional smile. "*How can I help you today?*"

"*I'm here to submit my bankruptcy application*" I replied, my voice quieter than I'd intended. Saying the words out loud felt strange, as if I were confessing a secret.

The clerk didn't bat an eye. He simply took the folder, flipped through a few pages to make sure everything was in order, and handed me a small receipt. "*We'll process this within the next day or so*" he said. "*You'll get an email confirmation, followed by a formal letter in the mail*".

And that was it. I had expected something more, a lecture, maybe, or a stern warning, but instead, the process was surprisingly simple. I walked back to my car feeling lighter, as if a weight had started to lift from my shoulders.

The Email That Changed Everything

The next morning, as I sat with my coffee, my phone buzzed with a new email notification. I hesitated for a moment before opening it, my heart racing. The subject line was short but clear: **Bankruptcy Approved.**

I read through the email twice, unable to believe it was real. The message confirmed that my application had been processed and approved, and included a bankruptcy number assigned to my case. The words felt heavy but liberating. I had done it, I was officially bankrupt.

Later that week, an official letter arrived in the mail, reiterating what the email had said. Holding the paper in my hands made it feel real. I stared at the bankruptcy number printed at the top, a symbol of both an end and a beginning. I was bankrupt, but I was no longer trapped.

The Weight Lifts

Becoming bankrupt didn't feel like the failure I had feared for so long. Instead, it felt like freedom. The phone calls from creditors would stop. The letters threatening legal action would no longer arrive. For the first time in years, I could take a deep breath without feeling like the world was closing in around me.

That night, I slept deeply for the first time in months. It wasn't that my problems had disappeared, I knew there was still a long road ahead, but the suffocating pressure had been lifted. Bankruptcy had given me a chance to start over, a chance I never thought I'd have.

A New Beginning

When I woke up the next morning, the world felt different. The debts that had once defined me were now part of the past. I wasn't free of responsibility, I knew I had to learn from my mistakes and rebuild my life carefully, but I finally had a clean slate to work with.

I spent the next few days reflecting on what had led me to this point. Bankruptcy had once seemed like the end of everything, but it had turned out to be a new beginning. It gave me the space I needed to focus on what mattered: rebuilding my life, learning healthier financial habits, and finding peace in knowing that I had survived.

But what I didn't expect was the bigger surprise that followed, something I had never thought would be possible.

The Court Orders Looming

Before bankruptcy, the debt situation had spiralled so far out of control that multiple court orders had been issued against me. These legal demands had felt like the final nails in my coffin. There were orders from my landlord ready to evict me, from creditors who had escalated their demands to legal action, and even from my child's school over unpaid fees. Each court notice was another crushing blow, forcing me to appear in court to either settle the debt or arrange a payment plan acceptable to the creditor.

The pressure was unrelenting. The thought of standing before a judge, trying to explain my financial situation, had kept me up at night. What could I possibly say? That I was trying my best? That I simply couldn't make it work? Words felt useless against the cold weight of those legal demands.

Preparing for the Court Appearance

A week after I received the bankruptcy confirmation letter, I had a court date amongst several more looming. Despite being officially bankrupt, I wasn't sure what impact, if any, the letter would have. The fear lingered. I wasn't ready to trust that everything would suddenly work itself out.

That morning, I carefully folded the letter and tucked it into a folder along with all the paperwork I thought I might need. My hands shook as I got ready, a mix of nerves, exhaustion, and uncertainty. Would they accept the letter? Would I still have to negotiate? Would I be humiliated in front of a courtroom full of strangers?

The walk to the courthouse was long, and every step felt heavier than the last. I clutched my folder like it was a lifeline. By the time I arrived and stepped into the building, I felt stripped bare. There was nothing left of the person I used to be, the person who had once managed to keep everything together.

A Moment in the Courtroom

The courtroom was exactly how I had imagined it, cold, sterile, and intimidating. I waited for my turn to be called, my heart pounding so hard I thought everyone in the room could hear it. I stared at the floor, at the walls, anywhere but the faces of the others sitting in the room with me.

When my name was finally called, I stood up, clutching the folder tight. I walked to the desk where the court clerk sat, preparing my details before I would appear in front of the judge. He asked for my name, confirmed the debt case number, and began processing the paperwork. I couldn't look him in the eye, my nerves fraying with every click of his keyboard.

Then he glanced up and noticed the letter in my hand.

"*What's that document?*" he asked, pointing to the paper I had been holding like a security blanket.

My voice barely rose above a whisper as I said, "*It's a bankruptcy confirmation letter*".

I handed it over, my palms damp with sweat. The clerk unfolded it, read the first few lines, and suddenly his demeanour shifted. I could see it in his face, a small flicker of recognition, followed by something I could only describe as calm.

"*Madam*" he said, his voice even and clear, "*this letter confirms you are bankrupt. Any existing court demands are immediately annulled. The bankruptcy process now takes over all of your financial affairs*".

The End of a Nightmare

I blinked at him, struggling to comprehend what he had just said. "*What does that mean?*" I asked, my voice cracking.

The clerk's expression softened just slightly. "*It means you no longer need to appear before the judge today. This debt is now part of your bankruptcy. It's over*".

Over. The word echoed in my mind. I felt frozen in place, like my body couldn't quite process what had just happened. For months, I had been bracing for this moment, fearing it, dreading it, and now, with a single letter, it was over. The legal demands, the court orders, the looming threats, all of it swept away by the bankruptcy process.

I muttered a shaky "*thank you*" and turned to leave the courtroom, my legs weak and unsteady. Outside, the weight I had been carrying for so long finally began to lift. I sat on the courthouse steps, clutching the letter in my hands, and allowed myself to breathe. For the first time in years, there was no one demanding anything from me. No threats. No calls. No court orders.

I didn't feel triumphant, exactly. Bankruptcy isn't something you celebrate. But for the first time in what felt like forever, I felt free. And in that moment, freedom was everything.

What Comes Next

Walking away from the courthouse that day, I realised something important: bankruptcy wasn't the end of the story. It was the beginning of a new chapter. The mountain of debt that had crushed me for so long was finally being dealt with. It wasn't my burden to carry alone anymore.

I knew there would still be challenges ahead. Rebuilding my life wouldn't happen overnight. But for now, I could breathe, I could rest, and I could start planning for a future I hadn't believed was possible.

As I walked home, letter in hand, I thought about all the people who might be in the same position I had been in. I wanted to tell them that there's a way through, even when it feels impossible. Sometimes the hardest step is asking for help. But once you take that step, things can, and do, get better.

Chapter 7: A Step-by-Step Journey

From Approval to Financial Assessment

When my bankruptcy was finally approved, I felt an unexpected wave of relief wash over me. It wasn't euphoria, there was still so much to process and navigate, but it was a moment of clarity. The formal beginning of this process, daunting as it was, marked the end of my spiral and the start of something structured, something manageable.

Once my paperwork was submitted and approved, my bankruptcy trustee stepped in. At first, the idea of someone overseeing my finances made me uncomfortable. A stranger diving into the mess I had made? It felt invasive. But it didn't take long to understand their role wasn't to judge; it was to help. The trustee was there to ensure the process was fair, to make sure all the rules were followed, and to help me resolve my debts as smoothly as possible.

The trustee's first task was to assess everything: my debts, my assets, and my income. I sat through this financial evaluation, feeling like my entire life was being picked apart. But there was no way around it. This step was crucial, it determined what, if anything, I'd need to contribute during the bankruptcy period.

What Debts Are Covered and Which Are Not

One of the biggest lessons I learned early on was that not all debts are treated equally. Some debts were discharged immediately through bankruptcy, while others would remain my responsibility. That distinction was vital, and, honestly, a bit surprising.

The covered debts included:

- Credit card debt
- Unsecured personal loans
- Utility bills
- Unpaid rent
- Medical bills
- Income Tax debt

These were the burdens that had been suffocating me, and knowing they were covered brought an immense sense of relief. But there were debts that bankruptcy couldn't touch:

- Court-imposed fines or penalties before bankruptcy
- Child support payments

- Government student loans (depending on the country)
- Debts incurred through fraud

Thankfully, most of my creditors were covered. That gave me room to breathe, but I knew I still had to deal with some lingering responsibilities. It wasn't a clean slate, but it was a manageable one.

The Bankruptcy Timeframe and Extensions

Usually, bankruptcy typically lasts three years and one day. When I first heard this, I thought, "Ok, I can survive three years". But the reality was a bit more complicated.

If I didn't comply with the requirements, keeping my trustee informed about changes in income, for instance, or failing to provide accurate information, my bankruptcy could be extended up to five years. That warning hung over my head like a storm cloud, reminding me to stay on top of everything.

For those worried about contributions, the system is fairly straightforward. If your income is below a certain threshold, you don't have to pay anything toward your debts. That threshold is designed to ensure you can still cover basic living expenses. But if you earn more than the limit, a portion of your income goes toward your creditors.

At first, I was afraid this would discourage me from working, but it wasn't like that at all. The system didn't limit how much I could earn, it simply required a fair contribution if I exceeded the threshold. It was transparent and, honestly, reasonable.

Working While Bankrupt: A Surprising Reality

One of the misconceptions I had about bankruptcy was that I wouldn't be able to work. I thought I'd be trapped in some kind of limbo, unable to move forward. But that couldn't have been further from the truth.

You're fully allowed to work while bankrupt. There are no restrictions on how much you can earn, and for me, that was empowering. I needed to feel productive again, to have a sense of purpose.

During my bankruptcy, I threw myself into work. It wasn't just about earning money, it was about rebuilding my confidence. I even saw it as an opportunity to learn new skills and plan for a better future. Bankruptcy wasn't a sentence; it was a chance to reset.

What Assets Can You Keep?

Another fear I had going into bankruptcy was losing everything I owned. I imagined myself standing in an empty house, stripped of every possession. But the system isn't designed to punish you, it's designed to help.

There are certain assets you're allowed to keep, like:

Tools of Trade: If you rely on specific tools or equipment to earn a living, you are generally allowed to retain these items up to a certain value. For example, tradespeople can keep their tools, and writers like me can keep their laptops.

Household Items: Essential furniture, clothing, and personal belongings are protected. You won't lose your bed, dining table, or clothing.

A Vehicle: In many cases, you can keep a vehicle up to a specified value. This ensures you have the means to travel to work or meet daily responsibilities.

Knowing I wouldn't lose the basics I needed to function was a massive relief.

The Role of the Bankruptcy Trustee

The trustee became my main point of contact throughout the process. At first, it felt strange to have someone so involved in my financial life, but they were professional and clear about what I needed to do.

He explained everything, what was expected of me, how my contributions were calculated, and what steps I needed to take. It wasn't always easy, but knowing I had someone guiding me through made the whole ordeal feel less overwhelming.

A Global Perspective: Variations Across Countries

Please note that laws vary from country to country. The timeframe for bankruptcy, the assets you can keep, and the contributions you must make will depend on where you live.

For example:

- In some countries, bankruptcy may last longer than three years.
- Some systems place stricter limits on the income you can earn while bankrupt.

- The rules about student loans, child support, and court fines vary widely.

But the fundamental principle remains the same: bankruptcy is a structured, legal process to deal with unmanageable debt.

Moving Forward with Hope

For those facing bankruptcy, it's easy to feel like you're trapped with no way out. But the reality is far more hopeful. Bankruptcy doesn't take away your freedom, it restores it. It allows you to reset, learn from past mistakes, and focus on building a better future.

By the time my bankruptcy had fully begun, I realised it wasn't the end of my story. It was a new chapter, one where I could finally breathe again. For the first time in years, I could look forward with hope, knowing that I had the tools to rebuild my life, one step at a time.

Chapter 8: The End of Bankruptcy

The Letter of Release: A Moment of Euphoria

It came quietly, an unassuming envelope in my mailbox, like so many others I had received over the years. But this one was different. My heart raced as I opened it, hands trembling with anticipation. The words leapt off the page: "*You are hereby discharged from bankruptcy*".

For the first time in years, I let out a sigh of relief so deep it felt as if it came from my very soul. I had made it. The weight I had carried for so long, the shame, the constant pressure, the endless fear, had finally lifted. I stood there in my living room, holding that letter, and tears ran down my face. It wasn't sadness. It wasn't regret. It was pure, unfiltered relief. I was free.

The process had taken time, but it was worth it. I had served my period of bankruptcy and come out the other side. It felt like emerging from a storm into a bright, clear day. I had survived the worst of it. There was no more fear of phone calls, no more court appearances, and no more looming deadlines. This letter was the end of the darkest chapter of my life, and the beginning of something new.

The Lasting Record: The Reality of Bankruptcy's Shadow

As the euphoria settled, I began to consider what this newfound freedom meant. The letter declared me a discharged bankrupt, but bankruptcy itself does not disappear without a trace. There are consequences that remain, as reminders of what I had been through.

For starters, my credit record would carry the mark of my bankruptcy for up to seven years. Any lender who pulled my history would see it, there was no hiding it. I had learned to accept this as part of the cost of finding relief. Seven years might seem like a long time, but in the grand scheme of my life, it was just a chapter, not the entire story.

Even more permanent, though, was the inclusion of my name on the official bankruptcy register. This record, I was told, would be permanent. For all the years ahead, it would serve as a public ledger of the time I had declared bankruptcy. It was humbling to know that my financial struggles had been etched into a record that would outlast me.

But instead of feeling ashamed, I chose to see it differently. That record was proof that I had faced something most people fear and survived. I had confronted a seemingly insurmountable mountain of debt and found a way through. My name on that list didn't signify failure, it signified perseverance. I was not defined by my bankruptcy; I was defined by what I did next.

The Path to Recovery: A New Beginning

With the letter of discharge in my hand, I knew that I was free to start again. Bankruptcy had given me a clean slate, and now it was up to me to decide what to do with it. The years of struggle had taught me to be cautious, careful, and intentional with my money. I had learned lessons that could only come from living through such hardship.

The recovery process wasn't instant, of course. Rebuilding after bankruptcy takes time and effort, but it is possible. I began by making small changes, setting a budget, saving modest amounts, and learning to live well within my means. At first, it was hard. I still carried the emotional scars of the bankruptcy, and there were moments of doubt.

But time passed, and slowly, I began to see progress. My confidence grew with every small step. I learned how to manage my finances better and how to avoid the traps that had led me into debt in the first place. No more credit cards!! I made peace with my past mistakes, knowing that I was building a stronger future.

A Home of My Own: A Story of Hope

What might surprise people is that bankruptcy isn't the end, it's often the beginning. Five years after receiving that letter of discharge, I achieved something I never thought possible: I borrowed money to buy a home. Sure my interest rate is a bit higher due to the risk involved of lending to a discharged bankrupt but this is a price that I am willing to pay.

The day I signed the mortgage papers, I couldn't help but marvel at how far I had come. There had been a time when I thought I would lose everything, that I would never recover. But there I was, standing in a house that was mine. It wasn't easy. I had to work hard, prove myself, and show lenders that I was a responsible borrower. But I did it.

The house I now live in isn't just a home; it's a symbol of hope. It's a reminder that financial ruin does not mean life is over. Bankruptcy gave me the chance to rebuild, and I took it. It was my second chance, and I made the most of it.

A Message to Those Still Struggling

To anyone reading this who is in debt, overwhelmed, and wondering if they'll ever escape, I want you to know that there is hope. I know what it feels like to lie awake at night, to feel like you're drowning, and to wonder if you'll ever feel normal again. I know what it feels like to be ashamed, scared, and completely lost.

But I also know that you can make it through. Bankruptcy is not the end of your life; it's a tool that can help you reset and rebuild. Yes, it's hard. Yes, it's humbling. But it can also set you free. The day you let go of the shame and take that first step toward finding help is the day you begin to take your life back.

The road to recovery might not be easy, but it is possible. I am proof of that. My life after bankruptcy is not perfect, but it's mine. I have a roof over my head, food on my table, and a sense of peace that I thought I would never feel again.

The Future is Yours to Build

Bankruptcy taught me that life is not about avoiding failure; it's about how you rise after you fall. If you are struggling, know that you are not alone. There is a way out of the darkness. The future is yours to build, one step at a time. And when you finally reach the other side, you'll look back and realise how strong you really are.

But one of the most important lessons I learned was not to leave it too late. It's easy to ignore the warning signs when you're overwhelmed by fear or shame, but the consequences of waiting can be devastating. Act *before* the bailiff shows up at your door with an eviction notice, or the bank arrives to repossess your home. The saying "a stitch in time saves nine" may sound cliché, but it couldn't be more true when it comes to financial crisis. The earlier you face the problem, the more options you have, and the less painful the solutions will be.

For years, I let credit card debt oppress me. It felt like a weight on my chest, growing heavier with every swipe of the card. And yet, despite knowing it wasn't the answer, I couldn't stop. Credit was my drug, my quick fix to solve problems I couldn't afford to face head-on. Each purchase brought a fleeting sense of relief, but it always came crashing down when the statements arrived, showing balances I couldn't hope to repay.

When I finally filed for bankruptcy, a silver lining emerged: over the five years my bankruptcy was active, I was forced to learn how to live without credit. At first, it felt impossible. The withdrawal symptoms were real, I craved the comfort of a card, the illusion of having what I didn't truly own. But slowly, I adapted. I learned to save before I spent, to prioritise needs over wants, and to live within my means. It wasn't easy, but it was transformative.

By the time I exited bankruptcy, I was not only credit-free, I was also free of the craving. I no longer felt the need for a quick fix. Instead, I had developed a healthier relationship with money, one that was rooted in patience and planning rather than impulse and anxiety.

Looking back, I see that the lessons I learned during those five years were worth more than any material possession I could have bought on credit.

Bankruptcy was not the end of my story, it was the beginning of a new chapter, one where I took control of my finances and my future.

So, if you find yourself struggling, don't wait until it's too late. Take action now. The process may feel daunting, but it's far less painful than the alternative. And when you finally reach the other side, you'll not only be debt-free, you'll also be free to rebuild your life on a foundation of strength, resilience, and hard-earned wisdom.

As for me, I'm living proof that there's life and hope after bankruptcy. I'm not ashamed of my journey. It has shaped me into who I am today: someone stronger, wiser, and far more grateful for the second chance I've been given.

Today, as I stand in the modest home I worked so hard to call my own, I know this: the weight of my past no longer defines me. I am free to move forward and live the life I choose. And so are you.

Made in the USA
Coppell, TX
05 November 2026

11315632R00038